Page Turners

BEST FRIENDS

Margaret Johnson

Series Editors:
Rob Waring and Sue Leather
Series Story Consultant: Julian Thomlinson
Story Editor: Sue Leather

NATIONAL GEOGRAPHIC LEARNING | CENGAGE Learning

Australia • Brazil • Japan • Korea • Mexico • Singapore • Spain • United Kingdom • United States

NATIONAL GEOGRAPHIC LEARNING | CENGAGE Learning

Page Turners Reading Library

Best Friends

Margaret Johnson

Publisher: Andrew Robinson

Executive Editor: Sean Bermingham

Editorial Assistant: Dylan Mitchell

Director of Global Marketing: Ian Martin

Senior Content Project Manager: Tan Jin Hock

Manufacturing Planner: Mary Beth Hennebury

Contributors: Vessela Gasper, Jessie Chew

Layout Design and Illustrations: Redbean Design Pte Ltd

Cover Illustration: Eric Foenander

Photo Credits:

60 3841128876/Shutterstock

61 spirit of america/Shutterstock

ISBN-13: 978-1-4240-4650-8

ISBN-10: 1-4240-4650-5

National Geographic Learning
20 Channel Center Street
Boston, Massachusetts 02210
USA

Cengage Learning is a leading provider of customized learning solutions with office locations around the globe, including Singapore, the United Kingdom, Australia, Mexico, Brazil, and Japan. Locate your local office at:
international.cengage.com/region

Cengage Learning products are represented in Canada by Nelson Education, Ltd.

Visit National Geographic Learning online at **NGL.Cengage.com**

Visit our corporate website at **www.cengage.com**

Printed in the United States of America
3 4 5 6 7 8 20 19 18 17

Contents

People in the story

Heather Neal
a twenty-five-year-old fashion designer, friend of Gary and Michelle

Gary Harper
a twenty-five-year-old graphic designer, friend of Heather and Michelle

Michelle Peterson
a young mother, friend of Heather and Gary

Jennifer Miller
a twenty-four-year-old chef, Gary's girlfriend

The story is set in the city of Minneapolis, in the state of Minnesota in the USA.

Prologue

The race was about to start. Heather's friend Gary was standing next to her on the starting line. They were both in a running club, and the club had races every month. Michelle, another friend, was in the crowd, watching them.

"Go, Gary! Go, Heather!" she was shouting now.

Michelle and Gary were Heather's best friends. They met while they were all studying art and design at college. They were all in their mid-twenties now, but the three of them were still very close. Although Gary was her friend, Heather still wanted to beat him.

The starting gun went off. "Go!"

Heather began to run. She had a good start! She was ahead of Gary! But then, just before the end of the race, her legs started to get tired. Gary began to catch up.

At the finish line, Gary was fifth. Heather was eighth. Gary had a big smile on his face. "Hey!" he said. "Not bad!"

"All right!" Heather said. "Don't go on about it!"

Michelle came over. "Bad luck, Heather," she said.

"I didn't sleep well last night," Heather explained. "I'm not at my best."

Gary smiled at her. "Don't be a bad loser, Heather," he joked.

"It's true!" she said. "I just lay there thinking about everything I need to pack for my trip."

"It's hard to believe you're really leaving tomorrow," Michelle said.

FINISH

"Yes," agreed Gary. "All those countries! Great Britain, India, Australia! You're so lucky. I wish I was going instead of staying here in Minneapolis."

Heather looked at him. "Then, why don't you come with me?" she asked.

Gary looked sad. "You know why," he said. "I can't leave my job."

"I left mine," Heather said. "Traveling is important to me. More important than a job."

"You didn't like your job anyway, did you?" Michelle said. "It wasn't what you wanted to do. But Gary loves his." Gary worked for a design company, drawing designs for products for the home.

"I do," Gary agreed. Then he smiled at Heather. "Are you worried about going?" he asked.

Heather smiled back. Gary knew she always got worried when she made any changes to her life. "A bit," she said. "But I'm really excited too! I've wanted to travel for so long!"

"It's going to be amazing," Michelle agreed.

Neil, another man in the race, spoke to Gary. While he was busy with the conversation, Michelle turned to Heather. "I'm really going to miss you," she started to say. But then they both saw a girl looking at Gary. "Look at her!" Michelle said. "I think she likes what she sees!"

"Shh!" laughed Heather. "She'll hear you!"

The girl did hear. She turned around. "Sorry!" she said. "Is he your boyfriend?"

"No, he's my friend," Michelle told her.

The girl looked at Heather. "Then he's *your* boyfriend?"

"No," Heather said. "We're all just good friends."

The girl looked pleased. *"Really?"* she said, and when Gary finished his conversation, she went over to talk to him.

Michelle smiled at Heather. "That's Gary!" she said, and Heather laughed.

Chapter 1

Coming home

One year later

As she waited in line at the airport to show her passport, Heather was smiling. It was going to be so great to see her friends again! If only the line weren't so slow! *Hurry up!* she thought. *Hurry up!*

Then finally, she was through. With one bag on her back and the other in her hand, she began to look for Michelle and Gary. But there were hundreds of people everywhere and she couldn't see them.

Then someone called to her. "Heather!"

She looked over and saw them, waving at her. Heather laughed and waved back. She moved quickly through the crowd toward them. "Hey!" she said when she got near. "It's so good to see you guys!"

"Hi, Heather!" Heather put her bags down, and then Michelle put her arms around her and held her close. "I've missed you!"

"I've missed you, too!" Heather said. "How are Corey and Matthew?"

But Michelle didn't get the chance to reply about her young sons, because Gary was in the way. "My turn!" he said, and then he picked Heather up and did a little dance with her, right there in the airport. "Heather, Heather, Heather!" he said. "It is so good to see you!"

ARRIVALS

"Put me down, Gary!" she said. But she didn't really mind. It was so good to see him again!

"I've got so much to tell you both."

"We can't wait to hear it all!" said Michelle. "And you'd better have photos."

"Oh, yes," laughed Heather. "I have photos. Thousands of them! Oh, Michelle, Australia was so great! You have got to go there some time. Tell that husband of yours he has to take you! The boys would love it, too."

"Come on," said Gary, "let's get out of here." He took her bags from her and walked ahead. Her bags were heavy, but they were no trouble for Gary.

Behind him, Michelle put her arm around Heather again, and they walked along like that. Heather felt happy. *I'm home!* she thought. It felt good.

Then she noticed someone waving at them. It was a girl, a pretty girl with long, dark hair. To her surprise, Gary waved back. Then he moved in the girl's direction. "Who's that?" Heather asked Michelle.

"That's Jennifer," Michelle told her, "Gary's new girlfriend."

"Oh," said Heather. As she watched the girl, some of her sunny feeling went away. She wanted it to be just the three of them. *And since when did Gary have a new girlfriend anyway?* she wondered.

Gary was bringing Jennifer over. "Heather," he said, "this is Jennifer, my girlfriend. Jennifer, this is my good friend Heather."

Heather smiled. "Hello, Jennifer," she said.

"Hello, Heather," Jennifer said, but she didn't smile as she spoke; she just looked at Heather.

She's looking at me as if she doesn't like me! thought Heather. *Why? She doesn't even know me!*

For a moment, there was a difficult silence. Then Michelle said, "Come on, let's get Heather home, Gary. She must be so tired."

"Yes," said Gary. "Of course. How long is it from Australia, Heather?"

"Around 16 hours," replied Heather. "With two stops."

"That's quite a journey!" Gary moved off again with her bags, and the four of them left the airport building.

When they got to the car, Gary put her bag away. Then Jennifer got in the front next to Gary, and Heather got in the back with Michelle. It was quiet in the car—too quiet.

"Where are Corey and Matthew today?" she asked Michelle.

"Pete took them to the park," Michelle told her. "They can't wait to see you."

Heather smiled. "I can't wait to see them either," she said. "I bought them some presents."

"I think they're hoping for presents," Michelle smiled. "I have orders to invite you to the house as soon as possible. Is tomorrow night OK?"

Heather laughed. "Tomorrow night is fine," she said. Then she made an effort to be friendly to Jennifer. "How did you and Gary meet, Jennifer?" she asked.

Jennifer didn't turn around to look at her. "We met at a party three months ago," she answered.

Three months ago? Heather found it hard to believe. *Why didn't you tell me about Jennifer in your emails, Gary?* she thought.

Jennifer was still speaking. "Gary got some of his drink on my dress," she said.

Heather laughed. "That sounds like you, Gary!" she joked. "Gary's always dropping things," she told Jennifer. "I remember one time he was carrying this big, special birthday cake." She looked at Michelle. "Do you remember, Michelle? It was for his mom's fiftieth birthday."

Michelle smiled. "I'll never forget it!"

Heather laughed and turned back to Jennifer. "Well, anyway, Jennifer, he was carrying the cake and . . ."

But Jennifer didn't let her finish. "Yes," she said. "His mom told me. He dropped it."

"Oh," said Heather. "Yes, that's right, he did."

"That was years ago!" Gary said. "Can we all just forget about it now, please?"

It was warm in the car, and the sun was bright. Heather closed her eyes for a moment.

"Wake up, Heather, we're almost back," Gary said.

Heather opened her eyes. "I wasn't asleep," she said.

Gary laughed. "You were," he said, "and I'm not really surprised. Sixteen hours is a long time on a plane."

Heather sat up in her seat. Were they *still* talking about her journey? Suddenly, Heather saw a large poster out of the window. There was information on it about a race in Minneapolis called the City Challenge. The City Challenge was fun. Teams had to run around the city answering questions. She and Gary always entered the City Challenge.

"The City Challenge!" Heather said enthusiastically.

"Great! I can't wait to start running again! I hope we aren't too late to enter for it, Gary."

Jennifer turned around in her seat to look at her. "Gary doesn't go running anymore, Heather," she said. "We go swimming together instead."

Heather felt shocked. *Was Gary really letting his new girlfriend tell him what to do?* "Oh," she said. "I see."

Chapter 2

Cooking and conversation

"You were away for a year, Heather. You can't expect everything to be the same."

The next day, Heather was sitting in Michelle's kitchen with a cup of coffee. Michelle's young sons were out in the garden playing with their presents from Heather. The sound of their happy voices was coming in through the open doors, and to Heather, the coral reefs of Australia already seemed like a dream.

Heather drank some of her coffee and looked at Michelle. "But I just don't think Jennifer is right for Gary," she said. "Do you like her?"

"She's a bit quiet," Michelle replied. "But Gary seems happy."

Heather remembered Gary smiling at Jennifer on the way back from the airport. "Jennifer doesn't even want Gary to go running anymore," she said. "Swimming? When did he ever swim? Gary really enjoys running!"

"Gary enjoyed running with *you*," Michelle said. "But you weren't here. So he found new interests. New friends. He's doing well at work, too. You know he's a manager now?"

"Yes, I know," replied Heather. "I'm pleased for him." She *was* pleased for Gary; she really was.

"When do you start your new job?" Michelle asked her now.

Heather smiled. "Next week," she said. "I'm really looking forward to it."

"You're going to be designing clothes for children, aren't you?"

"Yes. A real fashion design job at last! I can't wait! It's a long time since I learned to do it in college." She smiled at Michelle. "You're a mother. You can give me some advice!"

Michelle laughed and looked at her sons who were now lying on the ground outside. "Make the clothes strong and easy to wash," she suggested. "Those are the most important things for children's clothes."

Heather laughed. "I'll remember that!" she said.

They were silent for a moment, watching the boys. Then Heather said, "Gary's invited me to dinner tomorrow evening. I think Jennifer will be there too." She wasn't really looking forward to seeing Jennifer again.

Michelle looked at her. "She's really not so bad, Heather," she said.

◇◇◇

But the next day, as she stood waiting for Gary to answer the door, Heather felt nervous. She wasn't sure why. *It's only Gary,* she thought. *I've known him for years. There's no reason to feel nervous.*

Then the door opened and Gary stood there wearing a silly apron that made him look like a girl. Heather had to laugh. "That's a very good look on you!" she joked.

"Do you like it?" Gary smiled. "I'm hoping it will take your mind off the food."

Heather walked into the apartment, looking around.

She was pleased to see that it looked the same. Same old chairs, same old television, same books and pictures. Heather remembered so many happy evenings in this room, watching movies or just talking.

"I came early to help out," she said, following him into the kitchen. "What are you cooking?"

"I'm making pizzas," Gary said.

"You're *making* pizzas? What happened to takeout?"

"You don't just order takeout when your best friend turns up again after a year away!" Gary said. "You make an effort."

Heather looked around the kitchen. There were things everywhere, and nothing was ready. "Well," she joked, "if you change your mind about that takeout, I'm happy to go to the pizza store for you."

"This pizza," Gary told her, "is going to be the best pizza ever. It has to be; Jennifer's a chef. She likes good food." He pulled a chair out for her. "Now sit down and stop getting in the way," he said. "And tell me all about your travels. I want to know everything."

So Heather sat down and began to talk. And soon it was just like in the old days before she went away: she and Gary, laughing and joking, enjoying each other's company, forgetting all about the time.

"And so because the water was quite stormy, they told us to wear life jackets while we were swimming and looking at the reef," Heather told him. "Only the life jacket made it feel like I was on a boat."

Gary closed his eyes. He had a big smile on his face. "You were sick, weren't you?"

"Yes!" Heather laughed. "I was."

Gary laughed loudly. "Heather, you must be the only person in the world who can feel motion sick when you're swimming."

"I think you're right!" Heather agreed.

Gary smiled. "Do you remember that time on the boating lake?"

"When you made the boat go round and round? Yes, I remember that very well. I'm never going in a boat with you again!"

Gary laughed again, throwing his head back. Heather laughed too. And once they started laughing, it was difficult to stop. Heather was laughing so much, she almost fell off her chair. And *that* made them laugh even more. They were making so much noise, they didn't hear the apartment door opening. Neither of them realized Jennifer was there until she appeared in the kitchen.

"Hello," she said, and Heather and Gary looked up. "What's so funny?"

Heather stopped laughing and moved quickly away from Gary. The way Jennifer was looking at her made her feel as if she were doing something wrong.

Gary went over to kiss his girlfriend. "Just Heather being Heather," he said.

Chapter 3

A difficult meal

Heather tried to talk to Jennifer while they waited for Gary to finish cooking. "Gary says you're a chef, Jennifer," she said. "That's interesting! Where do you work?"

"At Umberto's Italian Restaurant," Jennifer said.

Oh! Heather thought, thinking about Gary's pizzas. "Italian food," she said. "That's nice."

Jennifer didn't reply.

"Have you been there long?" Heather asked.

"Not really," Jennifer said.

This is hard work! thought Heather as she tried to think of something else to say. "Do you live near your work?" she asked.

"Quite near," said Jennifer.

It was the same with anything Heather asked. Jennifer only gave a one or two word answer, and she didn't ask Heather anything at all. It seemed a very long time until Gary came in with the food.

When the pizzas finally arrived, they were a bit burnt. Jennifer left most of hers. Gary looked unhappy. Heather hated to see him like that. She knew how hard he'd tried with the pizzas. And she decided she was going to eat every bit.

"You don't have to eat it," he told her.

"One time when I was in India," Heather said, "someone stole my money. I was hungry for two days while I sorted things out. You don't forget something like that. Anyway, you went to a lot of trouble for us."

Gary was looking at her. His face was shocked. "You didn't mention anything about having your money stolen in any of your emails!" he said. "Why not?"

Heather looked at him. She wanted to say, "You didn't tell me everything in *your* emails either!" but she didn't.

"I didn't want you to worry about me, I suppose," she said quietly instead.

"My friend Lois went traveling," Jennifer said suddenly. "She wanted to meet someone and get married. Is that why you decided to go?"

Heather laughed. Then she realized Jennifer was serious, and that both she and Gary were looking at her closely. Her face went red. "No!" she said. "Of course not! I wanted to see the world and to have some adventures."

"Well," Jennifer said, "I guess Lois had adventures, because she met the man of her dreams in New Zealand. She still lives there; they got married."

"Wow!" said Gary. "That is some adventure!" Then he looked at Heather and said, "Did you meet anyone, Heather?"

Heather felt her face grow warm. Jennifer was looking at her too. For some reason, they both seemed very interested in her answer. She looked down at her plate. There was only a very burnt piece of pizza left now. "I met a few guys," she said, "but it was nothing serious." Then she put the burnt piece of pizza in her mouth and did her best to eat it.

The rest of the evening was just as difficult. When Heather sat next to Gary on the sofa, Jennifer didn't look very happy about it. "Can I sit next to my boyfriend, please, Heather?" she said.

Heather went red and got up to move to the chair. "Of course!" she said. "Sorry!"

After that, Jennifer didn't say much; she just sat very close to Gary, looking pretty. *She's waiting for me to go so she can kiss him,* Heather realized. And suddenly, she felt really alone.

I need to get out of here! she thought.

Gary was in the middle of speaking about something—Heather didn't know what. He looked surprised when she got to her feet. "Sorry," she said. "I'm feeling really tired. Still getting over my travels, I guess. I'm going to have to go."

Gary looked at her. "Do you want us to drive you?" His face was worried.

No! Heather said quickly. "Thanks, but I'm fine." She put her coat on. "I can get a taxi. See you both soon. And thanks again for the pizza."

Then she left.

Outside, she didn't look for a taxi. She needed to walk, to move her legs and to try to make sense of her feelings. *What an awful night!* she thought. Then she remembered laughing with Gary in the kitchen. *"No!"* she thought. *It was good until Jennifer came! It was really great to see Gary again and to tell him about my time away. It was Jennifer who upset everything. Oh, why did he have to go and meet her?*

Chapter 4

Fighting talk

"It was awful, Michelle," Heather said when she called her friend the next day. "Jennifer wasn't friendly to me at all."

"Poor you," said Michelle.

"I know!" said Heather. "How can Gary and I continue being friends if she's going to keep being like that?" Heather's voice broke a little at that thought. "I wish I was still in Australia, Michelle, I really do!"

"You don't mean that, Heather," Michelle said. "What about your new job?"

Heather thought about her work. "The new job is the only good thing," she agreed. "It's just everything else that's so awful."

"Oh, Heather," Michelle said, "I can tell how upset you are."

Heather felt like crying. "I really am," she agreed. "And the worst thing is that Gary just can't seem to see how Jennifer feels about me. If our friendship meant anything to him, he'd be worried too!"

Michelle was silent for a while. When she finally spoke, her words took Heather completely by surprise. "Heather," she said. "Do you think your feelings for Gary might be changing?"

Heather's heart began to race. "What makes you say that?" she asked.

"Well, it isn't the first time one of Gary's girlfriends hasn't liked you, is it?" Michelle said. "They never like the amount of time you two want to spend together. Usually you just laugh about it."

Heather thought about it. "I know," she said. "But somehow this feels different. Maybe it's just because I was away for so long. Maybe now that I'm back, I just don't want to have to share Gary with anyone!"

She was joking, but Michelle didn't laugh, and suddenly Heather remembered being in Gary's arms at the airport.

It felt so good, she thought. *Like being home*. Was Michelle right? Had her feelings changed?

"People always think there must be something between us, you know that!" she said quickly. "But that's only because they don't think a girl and a boy can just be friends. Gary and I have *always* only been friends. Just like you and him."

"It's different for me though, isn't it?" Michelle pointed out. "I was with Pete when I met Gary."

"Well," Heather said. "What if there was no Pete? Would you feel differently about Gary then?"

"Probably," Michelle said. "He's very good looking. And he's a really nice guy. Yes. Why not?"

"Oh," said Heather, feeling surprised.

"Look," Michelle went on. "Did you miss Gary while you were away?"

"Yes," Heather said. And she remembered how happy she was every time an email arrived from him.

"I know Gary missed you," Michelle went on.

"Well," said Heather. "I hope he did! We're best friends! It would be strange if he didn't miss me!"

Michelle was quiet for a little while. Then she said, "When I met Pete, I thought about him all the time. I wanted to be with him all the time. I felt as if he knew me better than anybody else. That's how I knew he was the one for me. I still feel that way."

"Mmm . . ." said Heather thoughtfully. It was true that she thought Gary knew her better than anybody. And she did want to see him a lot.

Then Michelle continued. "And I wanted to be near him of course," she said.

Now it was Heather's turn to stay silent. But her mind wasn't quiet. It was very busy making pictures in her head of her in Gary's arms, his head very close, his eyes looking down into hers.

"Look," Michelle was saying, "I've got to go now, Heather. I'm taking the boys out. But do you want me to tell you my opinion first?"

"I'm not sure," said Heather nervously. "OK."

"Well, think about it. Are you in love with Gary? Because if you are, then you have to do something about it. If you don't, then you risk losing him. He'll choose someone else to spend his life with. And a wife certainly won't want the two of you to be together all the time."

Heather didn't speak. She felt too shocked by Michelle's words. *In love? Wife?* They were big words.

"Look, I really have to go now, Heather," Michelle said. "Call me later. And think about it, OK?"

Heather did think about it. All day. She kept seeing Gary

on his wedding day. Gary with a wife. Gary with a family.

In the evening, she called Michelle back. "I think you're right, Michelle," she said, feeling very small and scared. "I think my feelings are changing. I think . . . I think I do want to be more than just friends with Gary. But I don't understand. Why didn't I feel like this right away, when I first met him?"

Michelle didn't answer the question. She was too busy sounding excited. "So you think you really like him then?" she asked. "Like a girlfriend?"

"Yes," Heather said in a small voice. "But what do I do about it?"

"You have to tell him," Michelle told her.

Heather was worried. "But what if I tell him and he doesn't feel the same way?" she said. "Our friendship will never be the same!"

"That may be a risk you just have to take," Michelle said. "And anyway, what have you got to lose? Your friendship with Gary is already changing. Because of Jennifer."

It was true. Things were already different between her and Gary. "I feel so afraid, Michelle," she said in the same small voice.

"I know you do," Michelle said softly. "But love is always a little scary, you know."

Love! Heather was silent for a while. Then she said, "Maybe if I don't see Gary for a while, these feelings will go away. Maybe things will just go back to how they were before."

"Maybe. And maybe Gary feels the same way you do and is afraid to tell *you* about it. Think about that."

"But he's with Jennifer!" Heather pointed out.

"Yes," Michelle agreed. "He is. But that doesn't mean she's right for him."

"She *isn't* right for him!" Heather agreed hotly. "In fact, she's completely wrong for him!"

"Then maybe you need to fight for him, Heather," Michelle said. "Maybe you need to fight."

Chapter 5

A decision

Heather was pleased to start her new job. It gave her something else to think about. On her first morning, her boss showed her around and introduced her to the other designers.

Everyone was very friendly. And after such a long time away from work, Heather felt very happy to be doing something.

At lunchtime, she had a sandwich with a few people from her team. Somebody started talking about the City Challenge.

"Are you entering?" Mary, who sat at the desk next to Heather, asked her.

Immediately, Heather thought about Gary. "I don't know," she answered. "I want to."

"Well, some of us from work are entering. I know it's a race for two people, but we're going to try and beat each other! I'm sure we can find you someone to race with if you want to join us."

As she smiled at Mary, Heather was thinking, *I want to enter the City Challenge with Gary like always.* And she remembered Michelle's words, *Perhaps you need to fight for him, Heather!*

"That's really nice of you, Mary," she said. "But can I get back to you about it? I just need to check with a friend.

We usually enter the City Challenge together, you see." And she made up her mind to call Gary about it that evening.

Later, as Heather waited for Gary to answer his phone, she felt nervous. But when he did answer, he was clearly very pleased to hear from her. "Heather!" he said, with a smile in his voice. "How was your first day at your new job?"

She smiled. "It was really good, thanks," she said. "Everyone was very friendly."

"That's great," Gary replied. "It's so important to get along with the people you work with."

"Yes," agreed Heather. "We have the same interests. In fact . . . there's a team at work entering the City Challenge. Actually, they've asked if I want to join them. Only . . . well, *we* always do the City Challenge together, don't we?"

Gary was quiet for a moment. Then he said, "We do. But if you want to do the City Challenge with your new work friends, that's fine."

Heather didn't know what he was thinking. *Doesn't he care if I do the City Challenge with people from work?* she wondered. Then she heard Michelle's voice in her head again, *Fight, Heather!* "Well, the thing is," she said nervously, "I don't want to."

"You don't?" said Gary.

Be strong, Heather! Heather told herself. *You can do this!* "No, not really," she said. "I . . . I want to do it with you, like always. We . . . we're a good team."

"Yes," agreed Gary. "We are." He was silent then. While she waited for him to speak, Heather remembered Jennifer in the car on the way back from the airport saying, "Gary doesn't go running anymore, Heather." She guessed Gary was thinking about her, so she made herself keep quiet. He had to decide for himself.

Finally, Gary spoke. "Sure," he said. "Let's do it! Tell the work team you're taken."

Heather laughed. "OK!" she said. "I will!"

"Gary and I are entering the City Challenge together," she told Michelle when she called later.

"Great!" said Michelle. "It's a perfect opportunity to tell him how you feel without Jennifer around. Why don't you tell him by the end of the race?"

Heather wasn't sure. "Do you think I can?" she asked.

"Of course you can!" Michelle said. "Good luck!"

"Thanks," said Heather. She knew she would need it. She thought about it all evening. *What if he didn't feel the same way? Would she make a complete fool of herself? And worse still—would she even lose Gary as a friend?*

Chapter 6

The City Challenge

On the day of the City Challenge, Heather met Gary at the starting point. She had a new haircut and was wearing a little makeup. She knew she looked OK, but she felt scared.

Like her, Gary was wearing the light blue City Challenge T-shirt. He looked good in it. *I always knew Gary was handsome,* she thought. *But it never made me feel this way before. This is so strange!* Her heart was jumping, and she felt a bit sick.

But Gary was just the same as always. "Hi!" he said with a big smile. "Are you ready for this?"

Somehow Heather managed a normal smile. "Yes. I've got my phone, my camera, and a map."

"And some food and drinks?"

"Yes, those too."

Gary put his arm around her. He often did this. But now it made her dance inside. "We're going to win this, Heather!" he said. "I just know it."

I don't care if we win or not, Heather thought. *The important thing is that I tell Gary how I feel by the time the race is over. It may be the only chance I get with Jennifer not around.*

They joined the other teams to check in with a City Challenge official, and got their list of questions. Then it was time to start.

CITY CHALLENGE
CITY CHALLENGE
CITY CHALLENGE
NGE

There were ten questions or clues on the list. All the answers were about different places in the city. The aim was to work out where the places were and to get to them as quickly as possible. Then the teams had to get a photo at the place to show to the City Challenge officials. And sometimes they had to do a challenge—something difficult or silly—before they were able to move on. Heather and Gary always enjoyed these challenges . . . and the running. It was fun.

Gary read out the first clue. "The smallest restaurant in town to have breakfast. I don't know that one. Do you?"

"No," Heather replied. Then she remembered Jennifer's job. She didn't want to make Gary think about Jennifer, but she was a chef. "Call Jennifer," she suggested. "She'll know."

Gary gave her a strange look. "I'd rather not call her," he said. "She didn't really want me to do this."

Heather looked at him. "Did I make you two argue?" she asked.

"No," Gary said, but he was still looking strange. "Look, let's not talk about it, OK? We can use the Internet on my phone to find out about the restaurant."

Heather had lots more questions, but Gary looked as if he didn't want to answer them so she left it.

It didn't take long for Gary to find out the name of the smallest restaurant in Minneapolis to serve breakfast. Then they had to run through the streets to get to it. When they were there, Gary asked someone to take their photo with the restaurant sign behind them. Then they moved to the next clue.

"Hungry?" read Gary. "Go over the water to find this

very big piece of fruit!"

Gary and Heather looked at each other and smiled. They both knew what the clue meant. It was about a work of art in the Minneapolis Sculpture Garden, one of their favorite places. "How many times have we run past that?" Gary asked.

"Only about a hundred!" Heather laughed.

"Let's go!" Gary said.

I can tell Gary how I feel about him in the Sculpture Garden, Heather thought as she ran after him.

But as they drew near, Heather began to feel nervous. *This is it!* she thought. *I'm going to tell him, right after we have the photo!*

But when they had their photo taken, there was a challenge to complete before they were able to move on.

"You need to find six letters," the City Challenge official told them. "They make a word. It's something you need in winter."

They began to look. Heather quickly found four letters: L, O, V, and E. She looked at them and smiled. She showed Gary. "Look," she said. "LOVE! That's something you need in winter. Well, all year round, really." And she looked at him, hoping her feelings were in her eyes.

But Gary wasn't thinking about love. He was holding up two more letters: a G and an S. "Gloves!" he said. "You need to wear gloves in winter!" And he hurried over to the City Challenge official with their answer.

Heather watched him go. *Next time,* she thought. *I'll tell him next time.*

But at the next place, they both had to eat a plate of pasta

CITY CHALLENGE
CITY CHALLENGE

with no hands, using only their mouths. And at the next, there was a band playing very loud music. They just weren't the right places to say, "I think I'm in love with you."

The afternoon was passing quickly. Soon Gary and Heather had only one clue left.

"Climb up for a taste of Russia," Gary read. "That has to be the Moscow on the Hill restaurant! Come on!"

Heather's legs were tired as she ran up the hill after Gary, but she didn't really notice. She was going to speak to him now. She *was*.

Gary asked a waiter to take a photo of them in front of the restaurant. "It's a bit dark for photos," the waiter said. "I'll use the flash." He took the photo and gave the camera back to Gary.

Gary took a look at the photo. "Thanks," he said. "That's great. Come on, Heather."

He was running off again. She had to stop him! "Wait, Gary! I . . . I have to tell you something."

Gary turned. "What?" he asked.

Heather felt sick because she was so nervous. "I . . ." she started to say. But she didn't get the chance to finish, because suddenly it began to rain heavily. Within seconds, they were both really wet.

"Wait inside until the rain's finished," the waiter invited them. He had to shout over the noise of the rain.

Water was running down Gary's face. "Thanks," he shouted back, "but we have to get to the finish line. Come on, Heather, let's go!"

He began to run back down the hill, and Heather followed him. Then he turned to look at her. "What was it you wanted to tell me?" he shouted, but then they saw some other runners heading for the finish line. "Quick!" Gary said. "Let's try to get there before them!"

They beat those runners, but they weren't the first back. "We didn't win!" Gary said when they saw a lot of people there ahead of them. His face was wet from the rain. Heather wanted to reach out and dry it with her hand.

"Never mind," she said. "It was still fun. We always have fun together, don't we?"

Gary gave her a big smile and put his arms around her. "Yes, we do!" he agreed. "Except in boats."

Heather smiled at his joke. She was in his arms, and it was where she wanted to be. Suddenly she wasn't nervous anymore. "Gary," she started to say, but just then Gary saw someone in the crowd and waved. As he let her go, Heather looked up . . . and saw Jennifer standing there, watching them.

"Jennifer!" Gary called. "Come and join us!"

Jennifer. As Heather watched her approach, the light went out of Heather's day. Gary still didn't know how she felt, and now she couldn't tell him.

Chapter 7

A new plan

Michelle and Heather were in a city center café. It was a week since the City Challenge. Heather was feeling down. She was avoiding Gary, because she didn't want to see him with Jennifer, and she didn't know what to do about it.

"Do you want to go to a show at the Institute of Arts on Saturday?" Michelle asked her. She was busy eating the top of her hot chocolate with a spoon, and didn't look up. "It's of Chinese paintings. It looks good."

Heather smiled at her friend. "Yes," she said. "I'd like that. What time?"

"Well," said Michelle, "Corey has a swimming thing in the morning. So how about 12 o'clock? We can get some lunch in the café first."

"That sounds great," said Heather. "Will you bring the boys?"

"No," Michelle laughed. "I don't think so. I want to enjoy it!" Then she looked up from her hot chocolate. "Tell Gary about it if you like," she said. "I think he'd like it."

Heather didn't want to talk about Gary, so she just said, "I'll see." But later, on her way back to work, she had an idea and reached into her bag for her phone.

◇◇◇

Saturday was sunny. Heather put on a new summer dress to go to the Institute of Arts. She took a bus part of the way, then walked, arriving at 11 o'clock, an hour before

Hi! Want to come to
see some art with
me and Michelle on
Saturday?

Michelle was going to arrive. As she made her way to the café, she felt very nervous. This was it. She really was going to do it this time.

Heather took a deep breath and went into the café. And there was Gary, sitting on his own. Good. There was no sign of Jennifer.

Gary looked up and saw her. "Hi, Heather!" he said, smiling. "Where's Michelle?"

"She's running a bit late," lied Heather.

"Oh well," said Gary. "Let's have a coffee while we wait. How are you? I haven't seen you since the City Challenge."

Heather took the seat opposite him. "No," she said. "I . . . work's been busy."

Gary was looking good. He was wearing a blue shirt, and it made his eyes look deep blue. It was so good to see him, and yet at the same time it was so difficult, too. He was looking at her carefully, reading her face, and it was hard to hide her thoughts and her feelings from him. *But you don't want to hide your feelings from him this time,* she told herself.

"So," she said, "is Jennifer working today?"

Gary gave her a strange look. "I don't know," he said. "We broke up."

Heather's heart jumped. She looked at him properly for the first time. "Oh!" she said. "I'm so sorry, Gary!"

Poor Jennifer! she thought. And she felt really bad that a part of her was happy about the news.

"Oh well," Gary said. "I guess we just weren't right for

each other. I was glad when you invited me today actually. I haven't been here for a long time. I'm looking forward to seeing the show."

Heather quickly looked down. *Your plan's worked,* she thought. *Gary's here. You're alone with him. Now all you have to do is to say what you want to say!* She looked up at Gary, feeling sick with nerves. He was so important to her.

Gary was looking worried. "Is something wrong?" he asked.

"No," she said. "That is, yes . . . Actually, Michelle isn't running late. She said to meet at 12. I asked you to come early because . . ." Heather couldn't look at him. "Because I . . ." She broke off and took a deep breath. Then finally, she looked up. "Because I have something I need to tell you," she said.

There, it was out in the open. Now all she had to do was to actually say the words.

Gary was looking at her. He was half smiling. "This is all very serious!" he joked.

He has no idea what I'm about to say, Heather thought, looking at him. *It hasn't entered his head.* The sick feeling in her stomach increased, and she looked down at her hands on the table.

"Heather?" Gary said. "I'm getting worried now. You aren't going away again, are you?"

If only it was just that! "No," she said. "It's not that."

"What then?"

Somehow, Heather managed to look up. "It's . . . it's just that . . . my . . . feelings have changed," she said. "I don't just want to be friends with you anymore. I . . . I'm in love with you, Gary."

The silence that followed her words probably only lasted for a few seconds, but to Heather those seconds felt like hours. As she sat there waiting for him to speak, she couldn't look at him.

"Heather," Gary started to say, but then someone else was speaking—a man.

"Gary!" he said. "So this is where you get to on your days off! And this lovely lady must be Jennifer!"

Jennifer! Heather's face went red as she looked up.

"No, sir," Gary said quickly. "This is my good friend, Heather. Heather, this is my boss, Mark Crawford."

"Oh, sorry, Heather," Gary's boss said. "Gary talks about Jennifer quite a lot at work, you see. But I'm very happy to meet you." Then he stood and spoke to Gary about work for a while.

Heather didn't listen. She just sat and waited for him to go. And all the time she felt sick as she remembered Gary's introduction of her. "This is my good friend, Heather." Good friend. *This was such a big mistake!* she thought. *Gary doesn't feel the same way I do at all!*

And suddenly she wanted very badly to go home. She wanted to shut the door of her apartment and turn her phone off. When she pushed her chair back and stood up, both men stopped talking to look at her. "Excuse me," Heather said. "I . . . just remembered something." Then she picked up her bag and walked out.

"Heather!" Gary called after her, but Heather kept on going.

Chapter 8

Time for truth

Gary caught up with her in the long line of trees outside the building.

"Heather!" he shouted. "Wait!"

Heather didn't slow down.

"Heather!" he shouted again. "Will you just wait?"

Heather stopped, her back to him. She was breathing hard, and her head was down to hide her face. Gary moved to stand in front of her and took hold of her hands. She still couldn't look at him.

"Heather," Gary said softly. "Are you all right?"

She didn't look up. "I told you I'm in love with you, but you introduced me to your boss as your friend. How do you think I am?"

"Heather," Gary said quietly. "You *are* my friend. My very good friend. And I really hope you always will be."

Heather closed her eyes tight. She felt the pain of his words right through her body.

But then he said, "But that doesn't mean I don't want you to be anything else. It doesn't mean that. Just lately I haven't thought . . ." He broke off. "Heather," he said, and his voice was very quiet and gentle. "Please, look at me."

Slowly, Heather turned her face up toward his. And what she saw there gave her a little hope. Because surely, that

was love she could see in his eyes? Oh, she knew already that Gary loved her . . . as a friend. But, wasn't this different? The way he was noticing every little thing about what he saw? That special light in his eyes? Could it be true? Could he really feel the same way she did?

Suddenly, it was all too much for her, and she began to cry.

Immediately, Gary took her into his arms. "Ah, Heather," he said softly. "Please don't cry."

But she couldn't stop.

Gary carried on speaking. "Heather, I'm so sorry. I don't know why it's taken me so long to get here. But back there, in the café, it was as if a light went on in my head. Mark was going on about something, I don't know what. I didn't hear a word he said. I was just thinking that . . . well, suddenly everything made sense."

He pulled back to look into her face. "Heather, have you any idea how much I missed you while you were away?"

She managed a small smile at that, pulling back a little to dry her face with the backs of her hands. "Of course," she said quietly. "Because I missed you every bit as much."

Gary smiled. "I'm so stupid, Heather," he said. "I thought I was just feeling sad because my best friend wasn't around. But it was much more than that. It was like only being half a person. When I saw you at the airport . . . well, I was just so happy."

Heather just wanted to stand there and let Gary talk, but she knew she couldn't do that. There were things she had to say. "But you were happy with Jennifer," she pointed out. "When I came to dinner, you weren't thinking about being with me."

"Look," Gary said, "I won't lie to you. Jennifer and I were happy together. But after you came back, well, it was *you* I wanted to see. Jennifer wasn't happy about me doing the City Challenge with you, but there was no way I was going to miss that. I *wanted* to do the race with you. And because I did something she didn't want me to do, she was angry with me. I didn't like that much. She wanted me to agree not to see you so often, too. I didn't like *that* at all! Now I see she was right not to trust me. Maybe she knew better than I how I felt."

They were silent for a while. Standing in Gary's arms, Heather began to feel safe enough to let the happiness into her heart. Maybe, just *maybe* this was really happening! Maybe Gary really did want to be more than a friend!

She smiled up at him. "I tried to tell you about my feelings during the City Challenge," she said.

Gary thought for a while. Then he smiled. "Oh, you did, didn't you?" he said at last. "You made the word love in that challenge!"

"Yes! But then you went and found the other letters!"

Gary smiled. "I told you, I'm stupid."

They were both smiling now. "Then I tried to tell you outside the Russian restaurant," Heather continued.

"But it started to rain!"

They laughed, looking into each other's faces.

Then suddenly, Gary stopped laughing and looked down into her face.

"Why did this take so long?" Gary asked.

"Because we were happy as we were," she said. "And we were afraid of destroying something good."

Gary's mouth was very close to hers now. "Do you still feel afraid now, Heather?" he asked.

She smiled at him. "No," she answered. "How can I be afraid? When it feels so right?"

"Good," he said. And then he kissed her.

Review: Chapters 1–4

A. Match the characters in the story to their descriptions. Use the names in the box.

Jennifer	Gary	Michelle	Heather

1. __________ has two sons.
2. __________ met Gary at a party.
3. __________ is just returning from traveling.
4. __________ is a manager at work.
5. __________ isn't very good at cooking.
6. __________ has a husband called Pete.
7. __________ has a new job.
8. __________ has a friend in New Zealand.

B. Choose the best answer for each question.

1. When Heather and Gary race each other, __________.

a. Heather beats Gary

b. Gary beats Heather

c. they finish at the same time

2. When Heather returns to Minneapolis, who meets her at the airport?

a. Michelle and Jennifer

b. Gary and Michelle

c. Gary, Michelle, and Jennifer

3. Jennifer tells Heather that __________.

a. she and Gary entered the City Challenge

b. she met Gary at his mom's birthday party

c. Gary doesn't go running anymore

4. What is Heather's new job?

   a. a chef

   b. a fashion designer

   c. a manager

5. Heather makes Gary laugh when she tells him a story about ______.

   a. getting her money stolen

   b. getting lost in India

   c. feeling sick when she is swimming

6. Michelle thinks that Heather's friendship with Gary ______.

   a. is changing because Gary's feelings have changed

   b. will never change

   c. is changing because of Jennifer

C. Who said this? Choose the correct answer from the box.

Gary	Heather	Michelle	Jennifer

1. "Don't be a bad loser, Heather." ______
2. "You didn't like your job anyway, did you?" ______
3. "How are Corey and Matthew?" ______
4. "Gary's always dropping things." ______
5. "We go swimming together instead." ______
6. "She's a bit quiet. But Gary seems happy." ______

D. Complete the crossword puzzle using the clues below.

Across

1. Gary cooks Heather and Jennifer __________.
5. Jennifer works at a __________.
6. Minneapolis __________ is very busy.

Down

2. the country Heather has just returned from
3. Heather and Gary both enjoy __________.
4. Jennifer is Gary's new __________.
6. Gary is wearing a silly __________.

Review: Chapters 5–8

A. Number these events in the order they happened.

______ Gary's boss stops to talk to Gary at a café.

______ Heather walks out of the café at the Institute of Arts.

______ Heather and Gary take part in the City Challenge.

______ Heather tells Gary she's in love with him.

______ Heather starts a new job.

______ Heather asks Gary if he will do the City Challenge with her.

______ Heather invites Gary to the exhibition at the Institute of Arts.

B. Read each statement and circle whether it is true (T) or false (F).

1. Gary wants Heather to do the City Challenge with her new work friends. T / F

2. Heather and Gary have to answer ten questions in the City Challenge. T / F

3. Heather and Gary have their photo taken in front of a sculpture of a big bird. T / F

4. The weather is good during the City Challenge. T / F

5. There is an exhibition of Chinese paintings on at the Institute of Arts. T / F

6. Heather, Gary, and Michelle arrive at the Institute of Arts at the same time. T / F

7. Gary's boss thinks Heather is Jennifer. T / F

C. Choose the correct answer in italics to complete the sentences.

1. On the first day of her new job, *Mary / Heather's boss* showed Heather around.

2. Heather made up her mind to *visit / call* Gary that evening.

3. Heather brought a *guidebook / map*, her phone, and her camera on the City Challenge race.
4. Gary used the *newspaper / Internet* to find the answers to some of the questions during the City Challenge.
5. The second place Heather and Gary ran to was *Moscow on the Hill / the Sculpture Garden*.
6. *Heather / Gary* found the letters for one of the challenges first.

D. Answer the questions.

1. Who did Heather have lunch with on her first day in her new job?

____

2. What does Heather do to try to look good on the day of the City Challenge?

____

3. What word does Gary spell out at the Sculpture Garden after Heather spelled the word "LOVE"?

____

4. What food do Heather and Gary have to eat using only their mouths?

____

5. Where were Heather and Gary when it started to rain heavily?

____

6. Why did Heather ask Gary to meet an hour before Michelle was going to arrive?

____

7. Why was Jennifer angry with Gary?

____

8. Why did it take so long for Heather and Gary to understand how they felt for each other?

____

Answer Key

Chapters 1–4

A:
1. Michelle; **2.** Jennifer; **3.** Heather; **4.** Gary; **5.** Gary; **6.** Michelle; **7.** Heather; **8.** Jennifer

B:
1. b; **2.** c; **3.** c; **4.** b; **5.** c; **6.** c

C:
1. Gary; **2.** Michelle; **3.** Heather; **4.** Heather; **5.** Jennifer; **6.** Michelle

D:
Across:
1. pizza; **5.** restaurant; **6.** airport

Down:
2. Australia; **3.** running; **4.** girlfriend; **6.** apron

Chapters 5–8

A:
6, 7, 3, 5, 1, 2, 4

B:
1. F; **2.** T; **3.** F; **4.** F; **5.** T; **6.** F; **7.** T

C:
1. Heather's boss; **2.** call; **3.** map; **4.** Internet; **5.** the Sculpture Garden; **6.** Heather

D: Sample Answers
1. A few people from her team at work.
2. She gets a new haircut and wears a little makeup.
3. GLOVES.
4. Pasta.
5. At the Moscow on the Hill restaurant.
6. To tell him that she was in love with him.
7. Because she didn't want him to run the City Challenge with Heather.
8. Because they were afraid of destroying their friendship.

Background Reading:

Spotlight on . . . Minneapolis

The city of Minneapolis is in the state of Minnesota in the north of the United States of America. Minneapolis is sometimes called the City of Lakes. It lies on both banks of the Mississippi River and has over 20 lakes and wetland areas as well as lots of parks. Because there is so much water in Minnesota, going out in boats is a very popular thing to do.

The first people to live in the area were the Dakota Sioux, and the name Minneapolis comes from the Dakota Sioux word *mni*, which means water, and the Greek word *polis*, which means city. Around 390,000 people live in Minneapolis.

Some other interesting things about Minneapolis:

Minneapolis has a famous Skyway System, which is a collection of covered passageways that link 69 city blocks over 11 miles. This means it is possible to live, work, eat, and shop without going outside.

The shopping center in nearby Bloomington—The Mall of America—is the size of 78 football fields. It has more than 520 stores and a theme park.

The Minneapolis Sculpture Garden is the largest city sculpture garden in the USA with more than 40 art pieces. It is home to the gigantic fountain-sculpture *Spoonbridge and Cherry*.

The people of Minneapolis love golf. More people from Minneapolis play golf than in any other city in the country.

Think About It

1. Minneapolis, with its lakes and parks, has a lot for people who like to be outdoors. It also has a lot for those who like to be indoors with its Skyway System and The Mall of America. If you were in Minneapolis, where would you prefer to be?
2. Minneapolis has a lot of public art. Do you think public art is a good idea? What public art have you seen? Did you like it? Is there public art in your country?

Glossary

boating lake	(*n.*)	an area of water for people to sail on in small boats
bungee jumping	(*n.*)	an adventure sport where you jump safely from a high place, often down toward a river
challenge	(*n.*)	a difficult and interesting thing to do
chef	(*n.*)	someone who cooks in a restaurant as a job
coral reef	(*n.*)	an area of plants and rocks under the sea
fashion	(*n.*)	a style of clothing; the way people dress
friendship	(*n.*)	being a friend with someone
Great Barrier Reef	(*n.*)	a famous coral reef in Australia
gloves	(*n.*)	clothes for the hands to keep them warm or protected
institute	(*n.*)	a building where a society does and/or shows its work
journey	(*n.*)	traveling from one place to another
joy	(*n.*)	great happiness
officials	(*n.*)	people in charge of something
passport	(*n.*)	a document from a government that certifies one's identity and permits a citizen to travel abroad
plate	(*n.*)	something flat that we eat food from
race	(*n.*)	an event where people try to be faster than each other
sculpture	(*n.*)	a three-dimensional work of art
takeout	(*n.*)	food that you buy at a restaurant or store and take home to eat